D1028943

HIP-HOP Biographies

DR. DRE

SADDLEBACK
EDUCATIONAL PUBLISHING

YPB
Dre
Dre

Beyoncé   Nicki Minaj

Chris Brown   Pharrell

Sean Combs   Pitbull

Drake   Rihanna

Dr. Dre   Usher

50 Cent   Lil Wayne

Jay Z   Kanye West

SADDLEBACK
EDUCATIONAL PUBLISHING
www.sdlback.com

ISBN-13: 978-1-62250-928-7
ISBN-10: 1-62250-928-5
eBook: 978-1-63078-050-0

Printed in Singapore by Craft Print International Ltd
0000/CA00000000
19 18 17 16 15 1 2 3 4 5

Table of Contents

Timeline

1965: Andre Romelle Young is born in Compton, California.

1984: Dre joins the World Class Wreckin' Cru.

1986: Dre starts N.W.A with core members Eazy-E, Ice Cube, MC Ren, and DJ Yella. They released their first songs on their own label, Ruthless Records

1989: N.W.A releases the mega-hit *Straight Outta Compton*. Tyree, Dre's brother and best friend, dies during a fight.

1991: Dre and Suge Knight start Death Row Records.

1992: Dre leaves N.W.A. He drops his first solo album, *The Chronic*.

1992: Dre is arrested for beating up TV host Dee Barnes.

1994: Dre wins a Grammy for "Let Me Ride." He also leads cops on a high-speed chase while drunk behind the wheel.

1995: Eazy-E dies from AIDS. Dre and Tupac release "California Love."

1996: Tupac Shakur is murdered in Las Vegas. Dre and Jimmy Iovine start Aftermath Records

1997: Dre meets Eminem.

1999: Dre and Eminem release *The Slim Shady LP*. Dre also releases his second solo album, *2001*.

2003: Dre releases 50 Cent's *Get Rich or Die Tryin'*.

2005: Dre releases Game's *The Documentary*.

2008: Dre introduces his line of Beats headphones.

2012: Dre releases Kendrick Lamar's *good kid, m.A.A.d city* to rave reviews.

2014: Apple buys Beats for nearly $3 billion. Dre becomes the richest man in hip-hop.

Straight Outta Compton

South Los Angeles was on fire the year Dr. Dre was born. That was 1965. At the time, the United States was in the middle of a struggle for civil rights. Martin Luther King Jr. spoke to large crowds about the power of nonviolence protest. People went on marches and had sit-ins. They organized boycotts to protest unfair segregation laws. But they were met with violence.

A neighborhood in South LA, called Watts, hit the breaking point. A riot broke out in the streets. African American residents were sick and tired of police violence against them. They were no longer willing to live in terrible conditions. They were ready to do something drastic. In 1965, they looted and burned the city for six days. South LA was a war zone. The local police could not handle the situation. The National Guard troops had to be called.

South LA neighborhoods like Watts and Compton had been very different during the 1940s. That was during World War II. During the war, factories were working overtime. Everyone who wanted work had it. Back then, South LA had black-owned businesses and popular jazz clubs. Many African Americans had jobs that allowed them to earn good money.

But after the war, the good jobs started to disappear. African Americans were hit the hardest. South LA was becoming a place with a lot of crime and poverty. The white police force in African American neighborhoods added to the tension. By the 1970s, South LA was at a low point. The community had few jobs, poor schools, and violent gangs. This was Dre's LA.

Dre's California roots go deep.

Dre is short for Andre. Andre Romelle Young was born on February 18, 1965. His mother, Verna, was only 16 years old at the time. His father, Theodore, was only 17. The teenagers married when they realized that a baby was on the way. The ceremony was in the living room at Verna's parents' home. The next year, the young couple had another son, Jerome.

Verna and Theodore both dreamed of being professional singers. There was always music in the house when Dre was a kid. Theodore was in a local R&B group, the Romells. In fact, Dre's middle name, Romelle, comes from his father's group. Verna gave up her musical dreams to raise her children. Both parents held part-time jobs to help pay the bills.

One day, Verna noticed that baby Jerome's nose was bleeding. Verna panicked. She rushed the baby to the hospital, but it was already too late. Jerome died on the way. The doctors told her that Jerome had died of pneumonia. The family was devastated by the loss. It put a strain on the young couple's relationship. Verna and Theodore split up a few months later in 1968. They officially divorced in 1972.

Verna was now a single mother. She worked at an airplane factory. She sewed children's clothing for extra money.

Then Verna remarried. Her second husband was Curtis Crayon. They had two children together, Tyree and Shameka. That marriage failed as well.

Verna got married once more, this time to Warren Griffin Jr. Griffin had a son named Warren Griffin III, who became Dre's stepbrother. Like Dre, Warren grew up to be a rapper. He is known as Warren G.

Verna tried to hold her large family together. But she struggled. Verna had suffered abuse in her relationships. She drank to cover up the pain.

Rapper Warren G (Warren Griffin Jr.), Dre's stepbrother, standing with rapper Neb Luv and a friend.

If Dre's homelife was difficult, the neighborhood wasn't any better. By the time Dre was in middle school, gangs were running the street. The Crips and the Bloods were the two biggest gangs. The gangs dealt drugs and fought. They carved the neighborhoods of South LA into territories. It was kill or be killed if a gang member wandered onto the wrong turf.

Verna worried that the local school was not safe. She wanted to keep her sons away from bullies and gangs. Dre and Tyree transferred schools several times. Then Verna moved them to a safer school in the suburbs. Dre was bright but not interested in schoolwork. His attention turned to girls and music.

In high school, Dre transferred schools again. His mother thought a change of environment might help him perform better in school. He left Centennial High in Compton for Fremont High in South Central LA. It didn't change things. Dre rarely showed up at school.

When he was 17 years old, Dre learned that his girlfriend, Lisa, was pregnant. It looked like he was repeating his parents' life. Dre knew that his future depended on doing well in school. But it was too late. He had spent too many years not trying. His grades were not high enough to graduate.

He briefly attended Chester Adult School and enrolled in radio broadcasting. Bored and uninterested, Dre finally dropped out of school. He decided it just wasn't for him.

But there was a baby on the way. And now Dre was a high school dropout. He could see nothing but more failure in front of him. So he escaped into music and left his responsibilities behind.

Verna tried to protect Dre from the LA gangs.

Is There a Doctor in the House?

Verna's dream of a career on stage may have died. But her love of music had not. It filled the house. She had a large record collection that Dre explored. When he was around four years old, he started deejaying for his mother. She'd give him a list of records, and he would play them at parties to the delight of her friends. Dre grew up loving soul music, particularly funk. For hours and hours, he would sit in his room listening to bands like James Brown and Sly & the Family Stone. But his favorite was Parliament-Funkadelic.

Led by George Clinton, Parliament-Funkadelic was a unique group of musicians. They looked like cartoon characters from another planet. They played a style of music called P-Funk. It was soul music spiced up with Jimi Hendrix's acid rock. Some of their most well-known songs are "Atomic Dog," "One Nation Under a Groove," and "Flash Light." Parliament-Funkadelic got people up to dance. Seeing them live was an experience people never forgot. Dre loved their strange costumes and futuristic sounds. They were out of this world.

Verna could see how much Dre shared her love of music. She bought him a mixer for Christmas when he was a teen. Dre was excited. He spent all of his time in his room mixing records. Sometimes he even fell asleep with his headphones still on. He experimented with sampling, taking the back beats of his favorite songs and playing with them. By speeding up or slowing down a melody, Dre learned how to weave one song into another.

Soon, Dre was mixing records at parties around the neighborhood. There is an expression that goes, "When a door shuts, a window opens." Dre had shut the door to school. But through the opened window, he heard music.

Dre was inspired by the music of George Clinton's group Parliament-Funkadelic.

How was Dre going to get from a party DJ to the big time? Dre went to nightclubs to listen to the local DJs spin records. He would spend all night on the dance floor *pop-locking* to the music. And he studied how the DJ would rock the crowd. Eventually, he worked up the nerve to play at a club. He earned a regular spot as a DJ at Eve's After Dark in Compton. He called himself "Dr. Dre," in *homage* to his favorite basketball player, Julius Erving, better known as "Dr. J." Dre even wore a white jacket and stethoscope to play the part.

In interviews, Dre talks about the pleasure he got when he made the crowd dance. He loved to drop the right track at just the right time. There was no other feeling like it. In time, his mixing and *scratching* skills grew. His reputation as a DJ spread.

Alonzo "Lonzo" Williams was the owner of Eve's After Dark. He noticed Dre's scratching skills. Lonzo invited Dre to join his group of DJs, the World Class Wreckin' Cru. Lonzo also asked DJ Yella and the rapper Cli-N-Tel to join the group. Shakespeare joined the group after Cli-N-Tel dropped out.

The young "Doctor" Dre wore a white jacket and a stethoscope.

The Cru wore glittery suits like other popular groups at the time. They styled their hair in wet-looking perm curls. And they practiced their dance moves.

With a doctor in the house, they released a single called "Surgery." It sold 50,000 copies. Their first album, *World Class*, wasn't a big hit, but it introduced them to a larger audience. The World Class Wreckin' Cru was invited on a short tour with Rick James. James had had a megahit in the 1980s called "Super Freak." That song has very recognizable beat. It's been sampled on MC Hammer's "U Can't Touch This" and Jay Z's "Kingdom Come."

The Rise and Fall of N.W.A

The World Class Wreckin' Cru scored a record deal with Epic. The Cru immediately went to work on their second album, *Rapped in Romance*. On the album cover, Dre stands in the center of the group in a shiny red suit and slick-backed perm.

But Dre was disappointed with their music. Their sound was too soft. He was more interested in telling stories about reality in Compton. He felt the group was only imitating the styles of other popular artists, like Run-DMC. Dre wanted to be original and have control over his own sound.

During this time, Dre became friends with O'Shea Jackson, an aspiring rapper who lived nearby. O'Shea was 19 and, like Dre, had avoided gangs. O'Shea was in a music group called C.I.A. (Cru' in Action). O'Shea was known by friends and family as "Ice Cube" because he always kept cool. Dre recognized Ice Cube's skills as a writer. Dre asked him to write a song for the World Class Wreckin' Cru. Dre returned the favor by providing the music for C.I.A. The two friends decided to strike out on their own. They brought DJ Yella with them.

Dre and Ice Cube weren't just planning their next group. They had a bigger plan—to start a record label. That kind of dream requires a lot of cash. So they recruited a local drug dealer, Eric Wright.

Eric jumped at the chance because he wanted to get off the streets. Eric took the name Eazy-E. He wrote rhymes too. They started a new label called Ruthless Records. Eazy-E brought in his friend MC Ren. Together, they called themselves N.W.A (Niggaz With Attitude). By forming their own label, they had complete artistic freedom.

N.W.A pose for a photo with other rappers before their performance during the "Straight Outta Compton" tour.

N.W.A released their first album, *N.W.A and the Posse*, in 1987. Dre experimented with laying sounds of the LA streets like gunshots and car horns over classic soul beats. Eazy-E's single "Boyz-n-the-Hood" started to get major airplay on KDAY, the first radio station to feature hip-hop.

N.W.A sold records out of the trunks of their cars and the song became locally popular. "Boyz-n-the-Hood" told a graphic tale about rolling through the hood in an old 1964 Impala car. The boyz ran into into gangsters and police along the way. Eazy used his guns to settle disputes. He talked about slapping women and using alcohol and drugs. It was a raw look at street life.

In January of 1989, N.W.A released *Straight Outta Compton* with a bigger label, Priority Records. That got them a bigger audience. N.W.A had caught the attention of America. White youth were excited by the dangerous themes and the rebellious attitudes. People worried that they were making violence look glamorous. Women spoke out against the disrespectful language. Older African Americans were disgusted by their use of the n-word.

The songs were too hardcore for radio stations. MTV refused to air their music videos. MTV said N.W.A encouraged violence. The media called their music "gangsta rap."

N.W.A preferred to call their music "reality rap." They said the lyrics reflected the truth about their neighborhood. If it was rough, then the truth was rough. Even without radio play or music videos on TV, N.W.A was gaining popularity. The album became more and more popular. In six weeks, *Straight Outta Compton* sold 500,000 copies.

One particular song video stood out. In it, N.W.A puts the police on trial for their brutal treatment of young black men. They rap about officers slamming suspects onto the concrete during stop-and-frisk searches. They complain that police see all black men as gangsters. Each rapper steps up to the stand to tell the jury how they will fight back. They fantasize about shooting cops who disrespect them.

Needless to say, the police were extremely upset and angry. They said that the song put a target on their backs. The Assistant Director of the FBI (Federal Bureau of Investigation) sent N.W.A a letter warning them that their music was encouraging violence and disrespect for the police. People argued that the songs were art. They were just an expression of feeling, not a call to arms.

The warning from the FBI didn't slow the sale of records. It did just the opposite. The N.W.A album was more popular than ever. Within a year, *Straight Outta Compton* went platinum. Remember, this was before the Internet. And again, the music was banned from radio and television. The success of N.W.A depended on people handing the music to each other, person-to-person.

Then the violence got real. On his tour bus one night, Dre received a troubling message from LA. His little brother and best friend, Tyree, was dead. Tyree had gotten into a fistfight with local gangsters. In the struggle, his neck had been broken. Dre left the tour to return home for the funeral. He couldn't believe his little brother was dead. Tyree was only 21 years old.

From Ruthless to Death Row

After the funeral, Dre returned to the N.W.A tour. He was still grieving the loss of his brother. But there was also trouble brewing within the group. Ice Cube had written 10 of the 13 songs on *Straight Outta Compton*, but he felt that he hadn't received enough money from the record sales. He finished the tour and left the group in 1989 to start his solo career. Dre and Cube remained friends.

Ice Cube's first solo album, *AmeriKKKa's Most Wanted*, went gold in just 10 days. It sold two million records in just two months. As a result, Dre and the rest of N.W.A were feeling the heat to step up.

Dre perfected his production skills and provided the sound for the next two N.W.A albums, *100 Miles and Runnin'* and *Efil4Zaggin*. (Read the second title backward). Those albums included a long list of hit singles. Dr. Dre had three platinum albums under his belt. He was ready to move on from N.W.A.

Dre started Death Row Records with Suge Knight in 1991. Knight was an ex-football player. Some people claimed he had been a drug dealer with ties to the Bloods. Standing at 6'3" tall and weighing over 300 pounds, Knight was imposing. He worked as a bodyguard for N.W.A and had a reputation for violence.

Dre still had a commitment to Ruthless Records, which got in the way of moving on to Death Row. Eazy-E claimed that Suge and his crew threatened him with baseball bats and pipes so that he would sign over Dre's contract from Ruthless Records to Death Row. Suge and Dre ran Death Row Records together. Suge handled the business while Dre handled the music.

Earlier that year, in January of 1991, Dre saw Dee Barnes, at a party. She was a female TV host and his one-time friend. Dre was angry about an interview she had done with Ice Cube. In the interview, Cube dissed N.W.A. Dre was furious because he believed that Dee had encouraged Cube's disrespectful comments.

Suge Knight became Dre's partner in Death Row Records.

Dr. Dre was drinking too much and getting into fights. He was risking everything he had worked for.

Dee says that Dre grabbed her ponytail and smashed her face into a wall. Then he picked her up and tried to throw her down the stairs. She fought back and ran into a bathroom to escape. Dre followed her there and punched her in the back of the head.

Dee got up the courage to take Dre to court. Dre pleaded "no contest" to the assault charges. He was fined and ordered to two years of probation. He also had to perform community service and give a PSA (public service announcement) about non-violence.

This was not Dre's only run-in with the law. He was first arrested in 1987 for not paying parking tickets. He spent the night in jail. In 1992, Dre was convicted of assaulting a police office after a fight in a New Orleans hotel. A few months later, Dre broke the jaw of Damon Thomas, a record producer. He received probation for the assault. Although Dre had managed to avoid the gangs as a kid, his list of criminal charges as an adult was growing.

In 1992, it was reported that Dre got into a fight and was shot four times in his legs. The hip-hop doctor was wheeled into surgery. In 1994, Dre led the cops on a high-speed chase through the streets of Los Angeles. Dre was drunk and testing the limits of his new sports car. He spent eight months in jail and had to enter a rehab program for alcohol.

Dre knew that he had to change his lifestyle to get his career back on track. In an interview he said, "I was on the road to failure, for real." During his months in jail, he had time to reflect on his actions.

While Dre was in and out of trouble with the law, South LA was tearing itself apart. In 1991, a man named Rodney King had been severely beaten by four white police officers. They claimed he was resisting arrest. But the beating was caught on tape. The video showed the officers kicking and beating King with their nightsticks. King was on the ground. His hands were shielding his face. The video made news around the world. People everywhere were horrified.

The police officers were put on trial in 1992. But the jury declared that the officers were not guilty of using excessive force. The verdict was like a match dropped into gasoline. South Central raged. History was repeating itself. This is what had caused the Watts riots in 1965, the year Dre was born. But this time, the outrage was more intense, and the destruction was even more extreme. This was the police brutality that N.W.A had rapped about. Without justice, there would be no peace.

South Central burned for almost a week. It was like a war zone. President Bush called in troops from the Army, the Marines, and the National Guard.

The troops locked the area down. Many people were hurt and killed in the chaos. The damage caused by the rioting cost more than $1 billion. The images of the riots on the TV news shocked the nation.

After the riots, the Crips and Bloods called a truce. They vowed to put an end to black-on-black violence in the neighborhood. For two months, South LA was peaceful. But the peace was short-lived. If LA was a harsh environment before the riots, it was a wasteland after. Thousands had been arrested. Businesses did not rebuild. Living conditions were worse than ever.

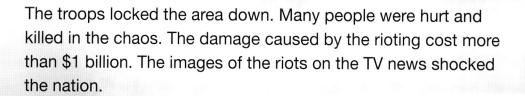

The police officers who beat Rodney King walked away without any punishment. The South LA community exploded in anger.

The Next Episode

LA needed a comeback. And in 1992, Dre offered some inspiration. He dropped his solo debut, *The Chronic*. On it, Dre rapped about what made LA so exciting: its women, its dangers, and its glory. *The Chronic* was a hit from coast to coast. Dre sold three million albums in 1993. Today, *The Chronic* is considered one of the best albums of all time.

The Chronic introduced Dre's particular brand of sound to hip-hop. G-funk blended gangsta rhymes, smooth rapping, and complex beats. G-funk combined record samples and live musicians. Listening to his mother's Parliament records as a child was paying off. Dre was making millions by expanding hip-hop's sound.

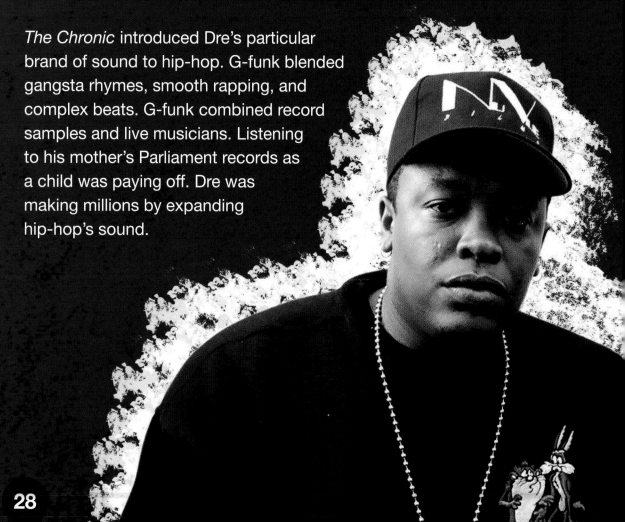

Dre's album also introduced Snoop Doggy Dogg to the world. Snoop was from Long Beach, the city right next to Compton. He was 21 years old, tall and skinny, and his rhymes flowed like melted butter. Snoop was so smooth! His voice went perfectly with Dre's grooves.

The two quickly became one of rap's best duos. They were the West Coast version of the Notorious B.I.G. and Puff Daddy. Like Puffy, Dre and Snoop achieved mass fame. In 1993, they appeared on the cover of *Rolling Stone* magazine. Dre and Snoop Dogg have worked together for more than 20 years. They've had chart-topping hits like "Nuthin' But a G Thang," "Gin and Juice," and "The Next Episode."

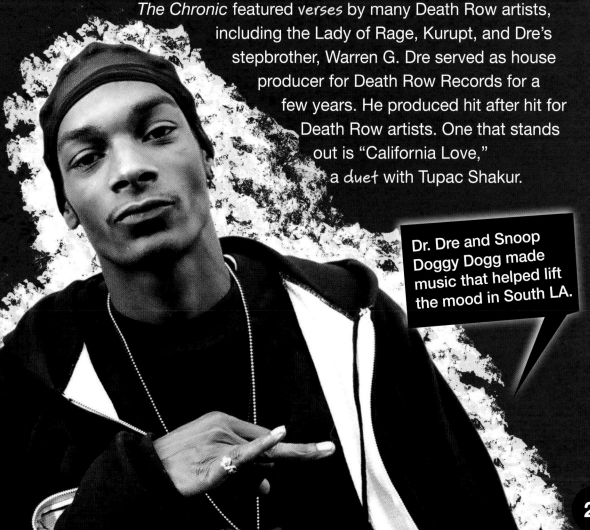

The Chronic featured *verses* by many Death Row artists, including the Lady of Rage, Kurupt, and Dre's stepbrother, Warren G. Dre served as house producer for Death Row Records for a few years. He produced hit after hit for Death Row artists. One that stands out is "California Love," a *duet* with Tupac Shakur.

Dr. Dre and Snoop Doggy Dogg made music that helped lift the mood in South LA.

To most people, Dre appeared to have it all. He lived in a mansion. He won a Grammy for Best Rap Solo Album. But to everyone's surprise, in March of 1996, Dre formally announced that he was leaving Death Row. He had his reasons.

First, Eazy-E had died from AIDS in 1995. When Dre heard that Eazy-E was dying, he had rushed to the hospital, but Eazy was already unconscious. Dre regretted mocking Eazy on songs and in videos like "Dre Day." He regretted letting his ego get in the way of his friendship.

Another reason Dre wanted to the leave was that Death Row had developed a reputation for violence. Dre was facing jail time for assault charges. Snoop Dogg was on trial for murder. Snoop was later cleared of that charge. Tupac and Suge Knight were publically trading insults with Puffy Combs and the Notorious B.I.G. of Bad Boy Records in New York. The media went crazy over the East Coast-West Coast feud. Dre was tired and afraid. He wanted out.

Dre gave Suge Knight the master recordings of his hits in exchange for his release from Death Row Records. After Dr. Dre left Death Row, the label quickly fell apart. Suge and Tupac were shot at in Las Vegas. Tupac died from his gunshot wounds. Suge ended up being sentenced to nine years in prison for violating his parole. His violent past had finally caught up to him.

Dre realized how lucky he was. If he had stayed at Death Row, he might have been in the car with Tupac. He might have been killed too.

Dr. Dre helped invent gangsta rap, but he chose to leave the gangsta lifestyle.

Dre's Aftermath

Dr. Dre reached out to Jimmy Iovine, the young owner of Interscope Records. Iovine took a chance on Dre. Together they started a new record label. Although Iovine was not a fan of rap music, he could see that Dre was an amazing producer. The high quality sound of *The Chronic* was impossible to deny.

Dre named his label Aftermath Records. Aftermath was a small label. Dre could take his time to find and develop talent. Dre had the opportunity to slow down and polish his skills. He was out to prove he could succeed without Death Row.

Aftermath got off to a slow start. Then Iovine gave Dre a tip that changed everything. He told Dre about Marshall Mathers, a white rapper who could battle toe-to-toe with the best. He went by the rap name Eminem. When Dre met Eminem, the young rapper was living in his mother's basement.

Dre quickly signed Eminem to Aftermath and went to work recording *The Slim Shady LP*. Dre brought the blond, blue-eyed rapper into the studio. And the employees at Aftermath thought Dre had gone crazy. But Eminem was no suburban wannabe. He had grown up in the slums of Detroit, Michigan. He was from a broken home and had experienced extreme poverty most of his life. The neighborhood he lived in had the same mix of gangs and violence Dre had experienced in South LA.

Eminem's flow like was no other. His rhymes were fast and dense. His stories were ridiculously funny and very violent. He rapped with a rage that reminded Dre of the early days of N.W.A. Dre had found a rapper who was skilled enough for serious fans and funny enough to attract a wide audience.

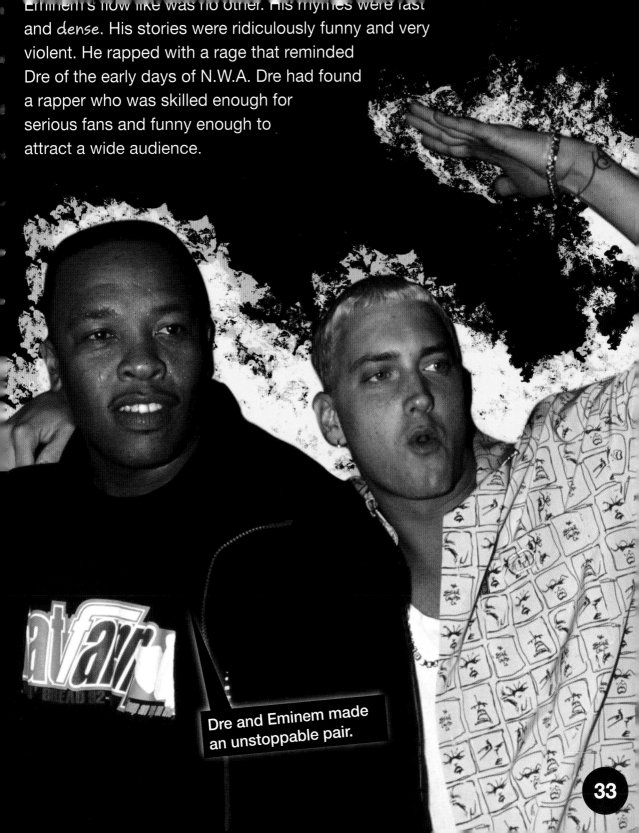

Dre and Eminem made an unstoppable pair.

Both Eminem and Dre have been criticized for their violent song lyrics.

Eminem's catchy hit single "My Name Is" took radio and TV by storm. *The Slim Shady LP* sold millions of albums. Suddenly, everyone knew who Eminem was. Teenagers across the country dyed their hair platinum blond and wore white undershirts to look like him. Eminem was a superstar. Dre was the man behind the music who made the magic happen.

Like N.W.A, Eminem wrote his fantasies of violence. His duet with Dr. Dre, "Guilty Conscience," told the outrageous story of three people planning crimes. On "'97 Bonnie & Clyde," Eminem rapped about getting rid of his wife's body with the help of his young daughter. The songs were disturbing. They were also clever. Eminem let his imagination run wild. He made no apologies for his outrageous songs.

Dre defended Eminem just like he had once defended N.W.A. The world is of full real violence. It is full of violent movies and video games. Why are violent songs so much worse?

Dre and Eminem continued to work together. Dre helped develop the young rapper's raw talent. Eminem released *The Marshall Mathers LP*, to acclaimed reviews. Dre and Eminem had created the album in just over two months. With Dre behind the board and Eminem freestyling in the booth, the two had a magic creative energy together. Eminem's rhymes were self-aware, vulnerable, and pissed off. *The Marshall Mathers LP* became the fastest-selling rap album of the time. Eminem was here to stay.

Dre and Eminem remained partners for years. Eminem learned from Dre, and in 1999, Eminem started his own label, Shady Records. Over the years, Dre and Eminem went on to create more top-selling albums together. They include *The Eminem Show, Encore, Curtain Call, Relapse, Recovery,* and *The Marshall Mathers LP 2.*

With his discovery of Eminem, Dre was back on top. The year after *Slim Shady*, Dre released his second solo album called *2001*. Ironically, the album came out in 1999. The album featured a host of big-name rappers including Eminem, Kurupt, Nate Dogg, Snoop Dogg, and Xzibit. In interviews, Dre talks about his constant need to prove himself to fans and critics. It had been nearly ten years since *The Chronic*. People wondered if Dre could still rap (fell off).

Dre proved that he not only had production talent, but was still one of the most original rappers in hip-hop. *2001* had a refined version of Dre's signature G-Funk sound from *The Chronic*. His rap style had also grown. On the song "The Watcher," he raps about aging in the hip-hop industry. He'd seen rappers come and go. He'd watch them get famous, then burn out. He'd watch them get rich, then lose their money in lawsuits. Dre was real. But he was also wiser. Since its release, *2001* has sold over seven million copies and is a hip-hop classic.

Dre does his best to keep his family life out of the news.

As Dre matured musically, he also discovered peace in his love life. Dre finally settled down with wife, Nicole Threatt, in 1996. They had two children, Truth and Truly.

Dre had been married before. And he had five children by three different mothers. There are rumors of more. Some of those family relationships were troubled. Dre was not there for his first son, Curtis, who he had fathered as a teen. In fact Dre did not meet Curtis until the boy was 20 years old. His second oldest son Andre Jr. died in 2008 of a heroin overdose.

Despite his fame as a rapper and producer, Dre is an intensely private person. He tries to keep his personal life out of the spotlight. He prefers to let his work speak for itself.

Dr. Dre was riding the bumpy waves of success. First came the highs. He went on the *Up In Smoke* tour and performed unforgettable shows with rappers like Ice Cube, Eminem, and Snoop Dogg. The highlight of the show was the N.W.A reunion with MC Ren and Ice Cube.

Dre's own album *2001* sold over six million copies. Another album that he worked on, Eminem's *The Marshall Mathers LP*, sold seven million copies. Dre was nominated for five Grammys in 2000. He won the award for Producer of the Year.

But there were also lows. George Lucas, the creator of *Star Wars*, sued Dre over a single sound. It's called the "THX Deep Note." Dre had asked for permission to use that sound on "Lolo." That's the opening track of *2001*. He was turned down. Dre says he recreated the sound in the studio. Dre claims that it was similar but not exactly the same.

The Fatback Band, a funk group from the 1970s and '80s, also sued Dre. They said that Dre had used a sample of their song "Backstrokin' " without permission. Dre had to pay a fee of $1.5 million to the band.

Dre joined a lawsuit against Napster, along with the band Metallica. Napster was created so that people could share music files online. This meant that people could download music for free. Dr. Dre was successful in protecting the music he owned. Some people think it's not fair to sample music and then complain about file sharing. But sampling and file sharing are not the same. Samples are used to make something new.

During this time, Dre also did some work in Hollywood. He took a small role in the film *Training Day*. He made tracks for popular films like *Above the Rim* and *Friday*.

Like other hip-hop producers, Dre was taken to court over using music without permission.

Keep Their Heads Ringin'

In 2003, Dre signed LA rapper Jayceon Terrell "Game" Taylor to Aftermath. Taylor was from Compton and was raised in foster care. Dre mentored Game for two years while the album *The Documentary* was released. While helping develop Game's sound, Dre also worked on Game's image. Dre promoted the new artist well. Even before any music came out, the hip-hop world had already been introduced to Game. Game appeared in music videos of other artists, Sean John ads, and television commercials.

Next, Dre signed Curtis Jackson III (50 Cent) to Aftermath. Like Eminem and Game before him, 50 Cent became a star. 50 Cent was well prepared. He studied with Jam Master Jay from Run-DMC. And 50 had serious gangsta street cred. He had been shot nine times. His first studio album, *Get Rich or Die Tryin'*, debuted at number one in 2003. The single "In da Club" was the biggest radio hit in history. In 2013, the album was certified platinum six times over and became the 10th highest-selling rap record of all time. Paired with the right rapper, Dre's hard-hitting music production was unstoppable.

Dre struck gold again with a young rapper named Kendrick Lamar. Lamar had been making mixtapes at home in Compton. After hearing Lamar's mixtape, *Overly Dedicated*, Dr. Dre knew that he had to work with the young man. Dre could relate to Lamar. They both came from the hood and understood its dangers. They had both avoided getting mixed up with gangs but sometimes found trouble anyway. They had both found a way out through music.

Dre signed Lamar to Aftermath in 2010. While performing onstage with Snoop Dogg and the Game in West LA, Dre crowned Lamar as "the new king of the West Coast." Together Dr. Dre and Lamar worked on Lamar's first album *good kid m.A.A.d city*. Many called *good kid m.A.A.d city* an instant classic. It went platinum in just a year.

Dre was responsible for introducing many new artists, including Kendrick Lamar.

With Eminem, Game, 50 Cent or Fiddy, and Lamar, Dre had created an all-star roster at Aftermath. Dre's artists were raw, vulnerable, and *explicit*. Dre's signature sound backed the hits of his crew.

Dre and Iovine got a huge payday when Apple bought Beats.

Dre had an amazing ear for sound. He knew quality when he heard it. And he would often make his artists repeat tracks until they were perfect. His excellent hearing led him to notice a problem in the music industry. For years, Apple's white plastic earbuds dominated the headphones market. But Dre was not impressed with their sound quality. He knew he could make a better product.

Dre teamed up with Jimmy Iovine (the owner of Interscope and the man who had introduced him to Eminem). The pair co-founded Beats Electronics in 2006. Their plan was to bring the quality sounds from the recording studios to music lovers everywhere. The company introduced stylish headphones, new software technology, and a streaming music service to the market. In 2014, Apple bought Beats for $3 billion. It was Apple's most expensive purchase to date. Dre's new business made him the richest man in hip-hop. He even surpassed Diddy. You might say that Dre took a bite of the big Apple!

Dre wanted to do something with the giant fortune he had earned. He decided that he wanted to give students the opportunity to learn the technical skills that had made him a star. Dre and Jimmy Iovine gave the University of Southern California $70 million to create a new program called Technology and Business Innovation.

The gift to USC was not the only generous gift that Dre has made. In 2001, he gave $1 million to disaster relief after the 9/11 attacks on New York City. It turns out that the man who defined West Coast rap has a soft spot for the East Coast after all!

Many people think Dr. Dre is the best hip-hop producer in history. He started Death Row and Aftermath. He has played a big role in creating two different styles of hip–hop—gangsta rap and G-funk. He has helped some of the greatest rap artists of all time reach their potential.

Throughout his career, Dre has been devoted to showing the reality of South LA. With N.W.A, he brought the sounds of the inner city to the rest of America. He told stories of the harsh realities of life in Compton. His lyrics told of police brutality, problems between men and women, and alcohol and drug abuse. The young audience loved the realness and rebellion. It made authority figures worry.

But Dre has also brought hope to hip-hop. His example shows that it is possible to move beyond the temptations and dangers of the street. His drive for perfection is well known. He strives for only the best and expects it from others. Where does this drive come from? In an interview Dre explains. He says that back in 1965, when he was born, teen motherhood was unusual. He said that everyone told his mother that she was ruining her life. They said that she would never amount to anything and neither would her children. Dre decided he needed to prove those people wrong.

Dr. Dre has not released a solo album since 1999. The hip-hop world has been waiting a long time for his third and final album, rumored to be titled *Detox*. With Dre's history, we know it will be worth the wait.

Dre had something to prove to those who said he would never amount to anything.

Vocabulary

AIDS	(noun)	a disease of the immune system that used to be deadly but now can be managed with medicine
aspiring	(adjective)	striving toward a goal
boycott	(noun)	an organized group of people who refuse to spend their money on something as a way of protesting
brutal	(adjective)	harsh and cruel
call to arms	(noun)	speech that persuades people to join a fight
to be convicted of	(verb)	to be found guilty in court of a crime
dense	(adjective)	woven closely together so that parts overlap
duet	(noun)	a performance for two people
explicit	(adjective)	describing things clearly, without any doubt
raised in / foster care	(noun)	a system of people who raise children in their home without legally adopting them
homage	(noun)	tribute or honor
ironically	(adverb)	in a way that is the opposite of what you might expect
jury	(noun)	the people in a court case that decide guilty or innocent
lawsuit	(noun)	court cases that settle disagreements
master recording	(noun)	the final recording that other recordings are copied from
mixer	(noun)	DJ sound equipment that makes a smooth transition from one song to the next
no contest	(noun)	a plea, or a statement, made in court that means you will not argue and will accept your punishment. It is not exactly the same as admitting you are guilty.

platinum	(noun)	a record that has sold at least one million copies
pneumonia	(noun)	an infection of the lungs
pop-locking	(verb)	a style of dance where you move like a robot or machine
probation	(noun)	a mild form of punishment that lets you stay out of jail as long you follow certain rules
R&B	(noun)	a style of music with soulful singing and strong beat. The initials stand for rhythm and blues.
rebellious	(adjective)	challenging authority
recruit	(verb)	to ask someone to join a group
rehab program	(noun)	a program that helps people get over an addiction to drugs or alcohol
resist	(verb)	to fight against
sample	(verb)	to use small pieces of music from other songs
scratching	(verb)	a beat made by using the needle on a vinyl record as it spins on a turntable
segregation laws	(noun)	laws that kept people apart according to their race
stop-and-frisk search	(noun)	a way of searching people on the street when police think that they are doing something illegal
street cred	(noun)	a quality of respect for someone who comes from the streets. Cred is short for credibility.
turf	(noun)	an area that is controlled by a gang
unconscious	(noun)	a state similar to being asleep but deeper
verse	(noun)	a section of a song that comes between the repeating chorus
vulnerable	(adjective)	showing weakness
wannabe	(noun)	someone who is trying to be something they are not

Photo Credits